Building a House Fit to Live In

Myra Richardson

DEDICATION

This book is dedicated to you the reader. Before you were formed in your mother's womb, Our Father which is in heaven knew your steps would get you to this book. It is understood that whatsoever we do in word and deed, do it unto the Glory of God. To God be the glory.

To my husband, children, sisters, brothers, my Greater Faith and Victory Worship Center family, and all those who believe in the God that is in me. Thanks!

CONTENTS

INTRODUCTION

To everything, there is a season, and a time to every purpose under the heaven: A time to be born, and a time to die; a time to plant, and a time to pluck up that which is planted; A time to kill, and a time to heal; a time to break down, and a time to build up; A time to weep, and a time to laugh; a time to mourn, and a time to dance; A time to cast, away stones, and a time to gather stones together; a time to embrace, and a time to refrain from embracing; A time to get, and a time to lose; a time to keep, and a time to cast away; A time to rend, and a time to sew; a time to keep silence, and a time to speak; A time to love, and a time to hate; a time of war, and a time of peace. (Eccl.- 3:1-8)

God has made everything beautiful in its time, or better, that there is an appropriate time for each activity. Time has a way of bringing about change. The keyword is change. The world is changing, and therefore the church too must change. When it comes to discussing change (renewal) there are probably three major classes among Christians.

First, some are ready to change almost everything but a doctrinal statement. These are those who have their thinking rooted much in the present. Then there are those Christians who are afraid of change. Change is threatening. Change is a bad word. In their minds, it is frequently classified as moving from their comfort zone. These people are those whose thinking, attitudes, and lifestyle are firmly entrenched in the past. These have developed security in doing things in a certain way. Because of their fears and uncertainties, these have even come to equate tradition with biblical absolutes. Going to church on Sunday morning and evening, and Wednesday night is almost as sacred to them as the "virgin birth," and "second coming of Christ."

Then there is another group-what we might call the biblical purists. These study the Bible carefully with little regard for either the past or the present. To them, culture and current needs are irrelevant, and studying history is a waste. The Bible is enough! "Expose people to the Bible," they say, "and God will do the rest." In one sense, all of these groups are speaking some truth…important truth! But in a broad sense, all are wrong, dead wrong! These have all missed the mark.

It is with these classes of people in mind that the Lord has spoken and said, "Every kingdom divided against itself shall not stand." Matthew 12:25

Nevertheless, through trusting in God, every house must be fit to live in.

MYRA RICHARDSON

1 ARISE

Key Verse - EXCEPT the Lord build the house, they labor in vain that build it: except the Lord keep the city, the watchman waketh but in vain. (Psalm 127: 1 KJV)

BEHOLD, the kingdom of heaven is like unto three servants who went forth to make houses for themselves. The first servant was walking along a way that seemeth right unto her when she met a man carrying a load of straw (anger, intellect, lust, and money). "Straw", thought the first servant. I can easily build a house of straw. It wouldn't take long or be much trouble. Therefore the first servant bought the straw and built herself a house. She lived happily in her straw house.

The second servant was walking along a way that seemeth right unto him when he met a man carrying a load of sticks (lies, lust, and pride). "Sticks", thought the second servant. I can easily build a house of sticks. It wouldn't take forever or be much trouble. Therefore the second servant bought the sticks and built himself a house of sticks. He lived happily in his stick house.

The third servant was walking along a way that seemeth right unto him when he met a man with a load of rocks. "Rock", (love, joy, peace, long-suffering, gentleness, goodness, faith, meekness, and temperance) thought the third servant. I can build a house of rock. It shall take long and be a lot of trouble. But when it is perfected it shall be a strong house. Therefore the third servant bought the bricks and set to work to build himself a rock house. It took him many, many, many days of mixing mortar to stick to straw to hold the rocks together and of laying the foundation and joining one rock to another. Day after day he worked by faith. The third servant was often persecuted. "Look at you, working so hard to build your house. If you chose our way you would have finished and we can party. The third servant replied, "from your perception this is true, but, when my house is perfected it shall be the measure of the stature of the fullness of Christ.

The persecutors hadn't thought this matter. Yet they persecuted and went their way. The houses are complete. Here comes the wind to test that which was built. The wind tried the first servant's straw house and the house was blown away. By grace did the first servant escape to find refuge at her brother's house made of sticks.

The servants shut themselves in the stick house and waited. Along comes the flood. The stream beat vehemently upon that stick house. Immediately it failed: and the ruin of that house was great. By grace did the first and second servant escape to find refuge at their brother's house made of   rock.

The three servants shut themselves in the house of rock and waited. Along comes the flood. The stream beat vehemently upon that house and could not shake it: for it was founded upon a ROCK. The first and second servants cheered. They perceived that they were saved now. The third servant said, "Help me because it's not over. We are saved by hope, but hope that is seen is not hope; for what a man seeth, why doth he yet hope?" (ROM. 8:24 KJV)

20 So I answered them, and said to them, "The God of heaven Himself will prosper us; therefore we, His servants, will **arise and build**... Nehemiah 2:20

2 SO, LET'S BUILD

Key Verses - *And the vessel that he made of clay was marred in the hand of the potter: so he made it again another vessel, as seemed good to the potter to make it. (Jer. 18:4KJV)*

Directions: Using the skeleton, connect each joint using scriptures that speak to you.

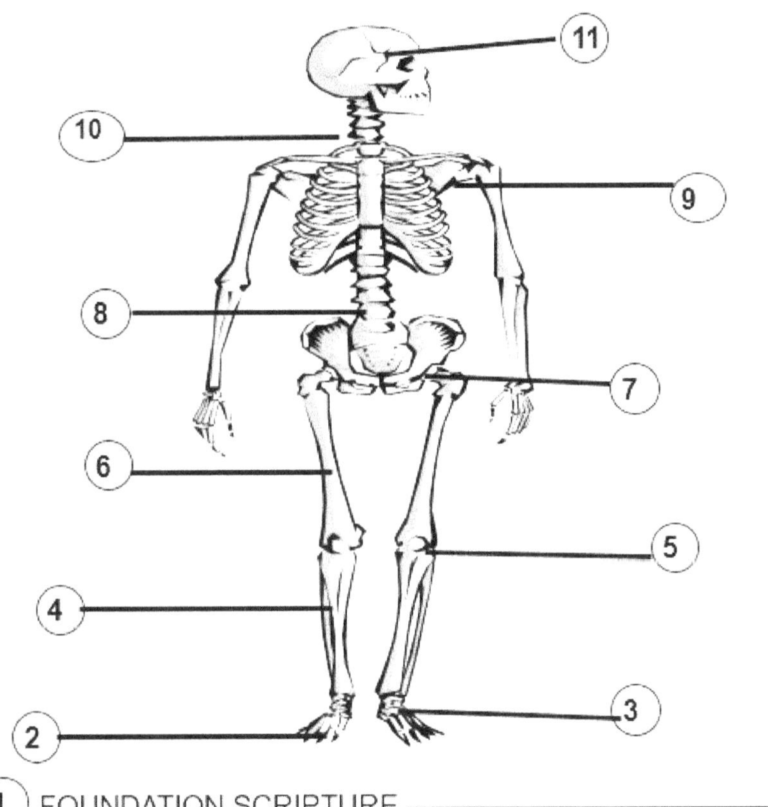

Key verse - *And he said unto me, Son of man, can these bones live? And I answered, O Lord GOD, thou knowest. Eze. 37:3 KJV*

1. Foundation-

______

2. Foot -

______

3. Ankle-

______

4. Leg-

______

5. Knee -

______

6.Thigh -

______

7.Hip -

______

8. Back -

______

9. Shoulder -

______

10. Neck -

______

11. Head -

______

3 UGLY

Key Verse – *O house of Israel, Cannot I do with you as this Potter? Saith the Lord, Behold as the clay is in the Potter's hand, so are ye in Mine hand, O House of Israel. Jeremiah 18:6 KJV*

When the tale begins, a mother duck's eggs hatch. One of the little birds is perceived by the other birds and animals on the farm as a homely little creature and suffers much verbal and physical abuse from them. He wanders sadly from the barnyard and lives with wild ducks and geese until hunters slaughter the flocks.

He finds a home with an old woman, but her cat and hen tease and taunt him mercilessly, and once again he sets off alone. The duckling sees a flock of migrating wild swans. He is delighted and excited, but he cannot join them, for he is too young and cannot fly.

Winter arrives. A farmer finds and carries the freezing little duckling home, but the foundling is frightened by the farmer's noisy children and flees the house. He spends a miserable winter alone in the outdoors, mostly hiding in a cave on the lake that partly freezes over. When spring arrives, a flock of swans descends on the now thawing lake.

The ugly duckling, now having fully grown and matured, unable to endure a life of solitude and hardship decides to throw himself at the flock of swans deciding that it is better to be killed by such beautiful birds than to live a life of ugliness and misery. He is shocked when the swans welcome and accept him, only to realize by looking at his reflection in the water that he has grown into one of them. The flock takes to the air, and the now beautiful swan spreads his gorgeous large wings and takes flight with the rest of his new kind family.

True love doesn't have to have a happy ending. True love has no ending.

True love is…

1 Cor 13:4-8

Love is patient, love is kind. It does not envy, it does not boast, it is not proud. It does not dishonor others, it is not self-seeking, it is not easily angered, it keeps no record of wrongs. Love does not delight in evil but rejoices with the truth. It always protects, always trusts, always hopes, always perseveres. Love never fails. But where there are prophecies, they will cease; where there are tongues, they will be stilled; where there is knowledge, it will pass away.

4 GREATER FAITH AND WORKS

Row, Row, Row Your Boat…

Imagine that you are in a boat that requires two paddles. One paddle is faith and the other is works. If you were to use only faith in building a house fit to live in, you would find yourself going in circles. Then again if you were to use only works the same is true. Faith and works go together like teeth and tongue. When using faith and works simultaneously, one will harness the energy and momentum required to keep moving forward. There will be challenges that will cause you to scream. And it is okay to scream… but keep building for great is your reward.

> *Row, row, row your boat,*
> *gently down the stream,*
> *Merrily, merrily, merrily,*
> *merrily, life is but a dream.*
>
> *Row, row, row your boat,*
> *gently down the stream,*
> *If you see a crocodile, don't*
> *forget to scream!*

BUILDING ACTIVITY

Directions: Take the letters of your name and create words
to describe who you are.

	Example A		Example B
M	Magnificent	M	Morals
O	Obedient	Y	Yippee
N	Nice	R	Remarkable
I	Intelligent	A	Ambitious
C	Creative		
A	Amazing		

Positive Word Cloud

<u>Building Relationships</u>

WEEK 1 CHALLENGE

CONTINUE saying POSITIVE WORDS and perform at least one unexpected gesture as an act of kindness.

Love is kind…
Be kind to one another, tender-hearted, forgiving each other, just as God in Christ also has forgiven you. —Ephesians 4:32

Please journal about your act of kindness:

____

____

____

____

____

____

____

____

____

____

____

____

WEEK 2 CHALLENGE

LOVE IS NOT SELFISH
Be devoted to one another in brotherly love; give preference to one another in honor.

—Romans 12:10 ...Whatever you put your time, energy, and money into will become more important to you. It's hard to care for something you are not investing in. Along with restraining from negative comments, make an investment that says, "I was thinking of you today."

How precious also are thy thoughts unto me, O God! how great is the sum of them! If I should count them, they are more in number than the sand: when I awake, I am still with thee. Psalm 139:17-18

Please journal about your experiences:

____

____

____

____

____

____

____

____

____

____

____

____

____

____

WEEK 3 CHALLENGE

LOVE IS THOUGHTFUL

Contact that special someone sometime during the week. Have no agenda other than asking how he or she is doing and if there is anything you could do for them.

How precious also are your thoughts to me… how vast is the sum of them! If Is should count them, they would outnumber the sand. Psalm 139:17-18

Similar to the building activity before, please take the letters of your significant other's name and create words to describe them. When finished, please share it with them.

How did it go?

____

____

____

____

Three-legged Race

Can two walk together, except they be agreed? Amos 3:3

A three-legged race involves two participants attempting to complete a short sprint with the left leg of one runner strapped to the right leg of another runner. The object is for the partners to run together without falling over, and beat the other contestants to the finish line. Find another couple and have some fun!

Please journal about your experiences.

You ARX Important

Instructions: Please do not think that you are not important in a relationship. While completing this activity page you should find that if one letter is missing then it like missing the U and R in CH_ _CH or the U in HO_SE.

- XVEN THOUGH MY TYPXWRITXR IS AN OLD MODXL, IT
- WORKS WXLL XXCEPT FOR ONX OF THX KXYS. I'VX
- WISHXD MANY TIMXS THAT IT WORKXD PXRFXCTLY.
- TRUX, THXRX ARX 42 KXYS THAT FUNCTION, BUT ONX
- KXY NOT WORKING MAKXS THX DIFFXRNCX.
- SOMXTIMXS, IT SXXMS TO MX THAT OUR
- RXLATIONSHIP IS SOMXWHAT LIKX MY TYPXWRITXR
- --NOT ALL MXMBXRS ARX WORKING PROPXRLY. YOU
- MIGHT SAY, "WXLL, I'M ONLY ONX PXRSON. IT WON'T
- MAKX MUCH DIFFXRXNCX."
- BUT YOU SXX, FOR A RXLATIONSHIP TO BX
- EFFXCTIVX, IT NXXDS XVXRY MXMBER ACTIVXLY
- WORKING. THX NXXT TIMX YOU THINK YOUR
- INVOLVXMXNT ISN'T NXXDEX, RXMXMBXR MY
- TYPXWRITXR, AND SAY TO YOURSXLF, "I AM A KXY
- PXRSON AND THXY NXXD MX VXRY MUCH."

Direction: Unscramble these positive words

Cteroopea	
orxyadirEntar	
osnteyH	
ssKi	
icaMigfntne	
penO	
mylaFi	
Knid	
esBdsle	
reisPa	
onseosdG	
bevLalo	
urCeosotu	
lPsiboes	
Pssboiel	
Jyo	
breealgeA	

Answer Key: Positive Words

Cteroopea	Cooperate
orxyadirEntar	Extraordinary
osnteyH	Honesty
ssKi	Kiss
icaMigfntne	Magnificent
penO	Open
mylaFi	Family
Knid	Kind
esBdsle	Blessed
reisPa	Praise
onseosdG	Goodness
bevLalo	Lovable
urCeosotu	Courteous
lPsiboes	Possible
Pssboiel	Possible
Jyo	Joy
breealgeA	Agreeable

WEEK 4 CHALLENGE:

LOVE IS NOT RUDE

He who blesses his friend with a loud voice early in the morning, it will be reckoned a curse to him. —Proverbs 27:14

Ask that special person in your life to tell you three things that cause him or her to be uncomfortable or irritated with you. You must do so without attacking them or justifying your behavior. This is from their perspective only.

Please journal about your experiences:

____

____

____

____

____

____

____

____

____

____

____

____

____

WEEK CHALLENGE 5:

LOVE MAKES GOOD IMPRESSIONS!

Greet one another with a kiss of love.
—1 Peter 5:14

...Think of a specific way you'd like to greet those special people in your life. Do it with a smile and with enthusiasm. Let's be determined to change our greeting to reflect our love for others.

Ex: Love, hug, good morning, hi, I love your smile, etc.

Please journal about your experiences:

____

____

____

____

____

____

____

____

____

____

____

____

5 PASS THE JOINT

From whom the whole body fitly joined together and compacted by that which every joint supplieth, according to the effectual working in the measure of every part, maketh increase of the body unto the edifying of itself in love. Eph. 4:16

The term 'relationship' is rooted in the word 'relation' and is defined as a mutual affiliation or connection between individuals or groups of people or entities. Relationships are built where there is mutual understanding between or among individuals. However, this is not built overnight. In a relationship, we must fight the good faith.

WE don't fight about what WE think WE fight about. It's not "the big five" identified in surveys: money, sex, raising the kids, in-laws, or house-work. WE fight when WE believe that someone doesn't care about how WE feel. WE fight about the pain of disconnection.

Fight is NOT full-blown physical encounters. NOT talking throwing plates and breaking skulls. NOT making your partner physically bleed or fearing for your safety. NOT bringing the police to your house. SIMPLY "arguing": two intelligent people finding themselves in the throes of healthy debate... **It means your love can survive anything.** If we don't fight with significant other, it just isn't real love. If we can fight, we have the power to survive. If we can say whatever is on our mind, even the most vicious of arguments couldn't tear us apart. If we can fight, we can make it. When we stop treading softly, we start growing closer.

- Fighting better is about having discussions, not arguments. It is about respectfully hearing the other person when problems arise. This will require us to present our bodies as living sacrifices, holy, acceptable unto God, which is our reasonable service. We cannot be conformed to this world, but be transformed by the renewing of your mind, that ye may prove what is that good, and acceptable, and perfect, will of God. For I say, through the grace given unto me, to every man that is among you, not to think of himself more highly than he ought to think; but to think soberly, according as God hath dealt with every man the measure of faith. Rom 12:1-3

- **Identify The Issue**:
  Husband likes to treat himself to little dinners out regularly, whereas Wife likes to save up for big treats. Neither is 'wrong' but this way you know where you both stand.

- **Localize, Don't Globalize:**
  Don't call up past arguments or offenses. it will only exacerbate an issue that is gridlocked (devolving into a larger fight).

- **Start With Agreement:**
  For example, if we have family coming in for the weekend and Wife wants a hotel, but Husband wants house-guests,

Wife could say, "I know we can agree that family time is important and I know we can both get a little annoyed when we are overrun with nieces and nephews. Let's try to think of a way to make this weekend work."

- **Look Underneath the Disagreement:**

Wife: I am mad as HELL right now.

Man: What now?

Wife: You aren't HELPING around this house.

Man: What are you talking about? I went to work this morning, did not I?

Wife: That is what I am talking about. You rather work for everybody else and do nothing at home. I am overworked and overwhelmed with the stuff that needs to be done.

Man: If you stop thinking that it needs to be done right now, then you won't feel overwhelmed.

Wife: At the end of the day it will all land on me.

Man: You shall have whatever you say.

Wife: I don't see you offering to help and that makes me mad as HELL.

Man: Why does that happen?

Wife: It makes me feel UNDER -APPRECIATED.

SOLUTION: Help and gratitude could be the ultimate healer in this fight.

- **Acceptance:**

    Knowing our issues and where WE stand can help prevent US from having the argument over and over again.

    Agreeing to disagree and naming the issue can prevent arguments in the future.

- **Success:**

  The more OUR issue is talked about, endured, and

  discussed, the easier and less trap-filled it will be.

6 COMMUNICATION ROADBLOCKS

For we wrestle not against flesh and blood, but against principalities, against powers, against the rulers of the darkness of this world, against spiritual wickedness in high places. Eph 6:12

Most of us pay attention to the way we communicate in the workplace, but when is the last time we really took inventory of the way we communicate at home? Although the home is the place where we should be relaxed and able just to be ourselves, it is also where those we love to reside. DO WE listen?   DO WE make ourselves available to our family members?

Without realizing it, we typically inject communication barriers into our conversation. Communication barriers are high-risk responses whose impact on communication is frequently negative.

QUICK TO HEAR AND SLOW TO SPEAK RESPONSES I

JUDGING THE OTHER PERSON

a. Criticizing: Making a negative evaluation of the other person, his/her actions, or attitudes.

"You brought it on yourself, you've got nobody else to blame for the mess you are in."

b. *Name-calling:* Is an attack on someone's self-esteem that results in defensiveness. A defensive person doesn't listen.

"You are just a bum, and you're always going to be a bum."

"I knew you were a slut when I married you and you are still a slut."
"Momma told me you can't turn a ho into a housewife, I should have listened."

    c. ***Diagnosing:*** Analyzing why a person is behaving as he/she is; playing amateur psychiatrist;

"I can read you like a book you are doing that to irritate me."

"Just because you went to college, you think you are better than I."

    d. **Judgmental *Praising* :** Making a positive judgment of the other person, his/her actions, or attitudes "Holier than Thou." "Mrs. Goody two shoe."

For in the same way you judge others, you will be judged, and with the measure you use, it will be measured to you. "Why do you look at the speck of sawdust in your brother's eye and pay no attention to the plank in your own eye? Mat 7:1-3

JUDGE NOT

A **judge** is a person who presides over court proceedings, either alone or as a part of a panel of judges. The powers, functions, method of appointment, discipline, and training of judges vary widely across different jurisdictions.

The judge is supposed to conduct the trial impartially and, typically, in an open court. The judge hears all the witnesses and any other evidence presented by the barristers of the case, assesses the credibility and arguments of the parties, and then issues a ruling on the matter at hand based on his or her interpretation of the law and his or her own personal judgment. In some jurisdictions, the judge's powers may be shared with a jury. In inquisitorial systems of criminal investigation, a judge might also be an examining magistrate.

QUICK TO HEAR AND SLOW TO SPEAK RESPONSES II

SENDING SOLUTIONS – often compounds a problem or creates new ones without resolving the original dilemma.

    a. *Ordering*: Commanding the other person to do what you want to have done. "Do your homework right now." "Why?!" "Because I said so. . ."

    b. *Threatening:* Trying to control the other's actions by warning of negative consequences that you will instigate. "You'll do it or else . . ." "Stop that noise right now or I will keep the whole class after school."

    c. *Moralizing:* Telling another person what he/she should do. "Preaching" at the other: "You shouldn't get a divorce; think of what will happen to the children." "You ought to tell him you are sorry."

    d. *Excessive/Inappropriate Questioning:* Close-ended questions are often barriers in a relationship; these are those that can usually be answered in a few words softened with simple yes or no. "When did it happen?" "Are you sorry that you did it?"

    e. *Advising:* Giving the other person a solution to her problems. "If I were you, I'd sure tell her off." "That's an easy one to solve. First…"

QUICK TO HEAR AND SLOW TO SPEAK RESPONSES III

AVOIDING THE OTHER'S CONCERNS – getting conversation off the track.

    a. Diverting: Pushing the other's problems aside through distraction. "ROLL TIDE ROLL"

    b. ***Logical Argument:***

    c. ***Reassuring:*** Attempting to convince the other with an appeal to facts or logic, without consideration of the emotional factors involved. "Look at the facts: if you hadn't bought that new car, we could have made the down payment on the house." Trying to stop the other person from feeling the negative emotions she is experiencing, "Don't worry, it is always darkest before dawn. It will all work out OK in the end."

QUICK TO HEAR AND SLOW TO SPEAK RESPONSES IV

Telling other people they are sending roadblocks:
When people are introduced to the roadblocks, a fairly typical reaction is, "That's just what my husband (boyfriend, girlfriend, mother, etc.) has been doing all these years. Wait till I tell him (her) about all the roadblocks he/she sends." Or, "Gosh, my boss uses just about all these barriers. The next time he/she does it, I'm going to point out how he/she is road blocking me."
This type of roadblock actually belongs in the judgment category

Know this, we can be angry but are not to sin, let not the sun go down upon wrath. Eph 4:26

Common perceptions and feelings that get in the way of communication and cause us unwarranted anger

We assume people know what we're talking about:

Closure point: Accept that people won't always understand what we saying.

Be patient and try not to get angry.

Be ready to clarify or repeat what we said differently.

We don't listen very well:

Closure point: The best way to improve our listening habits is to practice doing it better

Concentrate on what the other person is saying instead of our own thoughts and ideas.

Catch ourselves before we interrupt. If we're not willing to listen, Say *I-statements* to say so. For example, *"I'm not able to concentrate on what you're saying right now because I'm watching the football game. Let's talk later."*

We are not always clear about saying "no":

Closure point:

We have the right to say "no."

Ask for time to think when we need it so that we avoid feeling pressured.

Use *I-statements* to help deal with people who try to pressure us. For example, *"I'm not interested, thank you. I want you to quit asking me!"*

FOLLOW THE AUTHOR

Email: **mjrichardson37@yahoo.com**

Facebook: **facebook.com/myra.richardson.54**

YouTube: **Elder Myra Richardson**

Contact #: **205.554.RICH(7424)**